pretty broken

pretty broken

ANGEL PRATER

@angelprater
@prettybrokenpoems

Cover design by Angel Prater

ISBN: 9798703542316 (paperback)

this is the story
of how I've been broken
over and over again.
these are the thoughts
I had to get out
so that my heart could mend.

I wrote this for me.
I made this for you.

COVER UP

don't judge a book
by it's pretty little cover
cause a story not so pretty
might be what you discover.

TOGETHER

to tell you the truth
I wrote these for me
I never expected
anyone to see

but if there's even one soul
that feels less alone
from reading my words
that's an honor to know.

DOORS PT. 1

daddy's leaving
mommy's screaming
hide in my room
to keep from weeping

it never works
it only hurts
you tell him to leave
you shout
you curse

I beg
I plead
ear to the crack of my door
please don't leave tonight
please stay one night more

there's crying and shouting
then I hear the door slam
and the moment he left
I lost a piece of who I am.

DADDY'S LITTLE GIRL PT. 1

I get that adults
have their reasons
but having you there
was all I needed

how do you explain
to such a young age
"I have my reasons to leave
but you're not the reason to stay"

that takes such a toll
that's when it had begun
the terrible idea
that I was never enough

enough to stay
enough to choose
enough to fight
in the end I lose

maybe you assumed
that by 9 I'd be strong
that things would make sense
but man you were wrong

that's far from the truth
I know it hurts to hear
but the damage from you leaving
was incredibly severe

I waited
I was patient
the space in my heart
was sitting vacant

I thought about you
every day
I didn't understand
why you went away.

FAMILY PORTRAIT

family photo
an old disposable print
someone's face is scratched out
between them it's bent

this was a photo
of the love they now hated
it was just as disposable
as the camera that made it.

WALLS

when I was younger
I asked to paint my room
she'll pick a blue or beige
my mother did assume

but I went with dark grey
bought gold glitter too
and I mixed them together
and hoped it'd show through

taped all the frames
protected the floor
those boring old walls
I'd stare at no more

dip into the paint
and cover the wall
the color was dark
I had no care at all

cause a color too bright
just didn't feel true
to the lonely mess
that I was going through

I wanted my walls
to feel like my own
a great bit of darkness
with sparkle and glow

so I let the walls dry
and at first it would seem
they were plain grey walls
no glitter
no gleam

but when seen from an angle
at where the light hit
the entire wall sparkled
and I knew that was it.

there are some phone calls
you never wish to get
and when I was 10
my world altered quick

you can tell by the tone
when something's gone awry
the reason for that call
I'd never heard my dad cry

not a conventional cry
the messy kind
the only solution
when tragedy strikes

it was the moment he knew
he'd bury his son
and an eternity of sorrow
had only just begun.

we were both so young
when you were taken away
I couldn't comprehend
what happened on that day

so many mixed feelings
how does a 10 year old grieve
too many worlds crashing down
I was left in disbelief

but when everyone wore black
daddy sobbing by the pews
that tiny open casket
was enough to believe the news

I don't know what I thought
as I stared upon his face
but he gleamed a perfect angel
that could never be replaced.

spinning up
clouds break
they shatter in thin air
falling as we're spinning
intertwined pieces fly
bodies up fragments down
can we ever reach the top

spinning up
clouds break
immersed in a world of white
nothing pure but innocence
breaking and falling
torn from formation
bubbles burst
upside down
inside out
we're all so turned around

spinning up
clouds break
let the sunlight show
reflections from broken fragments
beam and illuminate
one breaks one shines
revealing all that's left behind

spinning up
clouds break
nothing is as it seems.

my mother was my hero
I thought she could do no wrong
she kept it all together
even after he was gone

she knew how much it hurt me
but she made sure every day
to tell me that she loved me
and she swore it'd never change

I started believing
I was enough
for atleast one
of my parent's love

cause maybe the bottle
took him away
but atleast my mother
decided to stay

I thought maybe my life
was turning around
just keep moving forward
no need to shut down.

COUNTDOWN

from 10 onto 11
you seemed happy
life was perfection

11 turned to 12
we met that man
you failed to mention

by 12 onto 13
he'd taken all of
your attention

13 going 14
I had a growing
apprehension

summer of 14 - 15
we had a family intervention

we sat gathered
in that room
I was shocked
as much as you

that idea
I thought was wrong
came flooding back
cause you were gone

going to rehab?
wait what you're an addict?
and in that room
I'd finally had it

the years I was left alone
they finally all made sense
you gave up way before then
and all at my expense

shoved into depression
so naïve and such a fool
I did everything you asked
you just used me like a tool

and in that room I cursed the heavens
what did I do to deserve this fate
the only two people I ever needed
chose their vices and walked away.

PRETTY BROKEN

yeah I'm pretty
pretty broken
broken plenty
plainly spoken

pretty see
so pretty me
to you I'm pretty
so that's all I'll be

but pretty's perfect
perfect cover
close the shutter
of vacant mother
buried brother
weakened father
troubled brother
hurtful lover
troubled other brother

but hey I'm pretty
that's all you see
but a pretty life
just wasn't for me.

how did you spend
your weekday nights
doing your homework
or Friday night lights

well my reality
was something I hid
went to meetings to support
her recovery process

NA or AA
doesn't matter which one
I didn't really mind
but it surely wasn't fun

don't get me wrong
these groups save lives
if you're committed
you might survive

all I wanted
was to be normal
but instead I felt
like a two-act performer

go to school
like nothing's wrong
I fall in place
like I belong

no one knew
why I moved there
I'm sure I lied
they were unaware

that it wasn't my choice
to be the new girl
to be dropped into
this brand new world

but I got to play
the typical teen
stucco spirit chair
captain of the cheer team

how ironic how my spirit
and cheer would disappear
the moment I went home
and my problems were so clear

you can't escape reality
no matter how hard you try
cause after cheer practice ends
you go to those same meetings at night.

ILLUSIONS

you see the way
I work the room
you see my strength
so you assume

you see the way
I lighten the mood
you see me happy
so you conclude

you see the way
I laugh with the rest
you see my smile
so you expect

but like an illusion
it's what I do
you see the things
I want you to.

WICKED BOOMERANG

the journey
the battle
I had put in the past
each time that it ends
I believe it's the last

but that's the thing about addiction
it's a wicked boomerang
you hope it won't come back
but some things never change

let me live within this moment
before it all falls down
to feel the heartbeat of my mother
the one I thought I'd found

took me years to open up
felt support I felt the love
close my eyes pray I don't lose her
pray to God that I'm enough

now I'm begging and I'm pleading
I can't lose my mom again
cause the loss of a child's mother
is a wound too hard to mend

I can't live in this childhood fantasy
it's time to open up my eyes
it's what I feared she's disappeared
tears stream down as my fantasy dies.

BRAT

friends think I hate you
cause when I see you I suddenly change
my calm and cool demeanor
seems to quickly melt away

I end up lashing out
then I really look like a brat
but if you knew the past and saw the mask
you might just have my back.

GLASS

have you ever stopped to look
at shattered glass on the street
you know something went wrong
something somewhere incomplete

a quick moment to admire
the shattered design
see my pieces in those pieces
I've shattered yet I shine

art imitates life
life imitates me
but everyone keeps walking
like there's nothing more to see.

the cruelest cycle
letting down
chained to sorrow
no holy grail

let you in
to let me down
I pray one day
you'll come around

empty words
but full of pain
my whole world stops
then falls like rain

how does it feel
to be a fiend
to need a high
like you need to breathe

you can't go without
that daily escape
every day that you hide
is a day that you waste

whether popping or sipping
chasing bottoms of bottles
I was raising my parents
my so called "role models"

I picked up the pieces
shattered long time ago
I let the wounds heal
still scars there that show.

FITTING IN

being thin
fitting in
with this mind
I'll never win

constant thoughts
of food and weight
eat me alive
with passing days

the shell of mine
it hides it well
clutching secrets
I'd never tell

what you see
isn't what you get
the monster inside
that I'm living with

without your own
you'd never know
without some help
he'll only grow

larger. louder.
he won't be stopped
you can't control
the ticking clock

it's time to eat
so pile it in
so I can make
you feel again

the guilt. disgust.
the growing shame
it never ends
his hopeless game

they call him Ed
is it me or him?
this awful voice
I met back then

being thin
fitting in
this ruthless game
I'll never win.

I don't want to feel broken
but it's all that I've known
all the lies I've been told
and the truth I've been shown

push the pain
far away
but it lives
as it may

make amends
with the past
I don't want
it to last

lingering
spreading
filling corners of my mind
let it seep to my heart
and it won't be too kind

so put the past
where it goes
somewhere dark
where nothing shows

but the dark
it haunts the light
we often fear
what's out of sight

so tucked away
is where it lays
but I still feel it
on broken days.

BIRTHDAY GIFTS PT. 1

on my 21st birthday
on august 21st
I got the greatest gift
and it came from mother earth

the great american eclipse
spanned across the USA
and on the line of visibility
the town I lived did lay

was it a coincidence
or an unbelievable gift
the moon moved in place
and I watched the world shift

perfectly aligned
the earth moon and sun
cast a shadow of darkness
day and night became one

the crickets chirped
the air grew cold
nature worked it's magic
I watched it unfold

for a split second
the sun and her moon
were finally together
wished to meet again soon

the reunion of distant lovers
I was positioned not to miss
nothing shows the bond of light and dark
like a total solar eclipse.

CALIFORNIA

from very young
I always knew
I'd somehow find
my way to you

I'd sit and dream
bout how we'd meet
to move so far
was bitter sweet

a great enough distance
to put from the past
with you I could thrive
build something to last

so right after college
I booked a one way
said my goodbyes
shipped my car away

I got on my flight
had a layover in Georgia
and it was love at first sight
when I met California.

33,000 foot elevation
still not enough of a separation

from my feet on the ground
to feel safe and sound

you can always run
can never hide
sometimes you can't
get out of plain sight

I'm flying away
from where I'm secure
I'm flying to where
I feel insecure

it doesn't matter my goals
or the plan in my mind
they're not on their agenda
I'm wasting my time

so just keep quiet
and keep your head down
you might avoid attention
if you never make a sound

my Leo turns to Virgo
a switch over the cusp
like going coast to coast
transition is a must

the extrovert turned
all the way in
cause I know this is a game
that I'll never win

my competitive edge
waves the white flag
surrendering in silence
is the best chance I have

anxiety growing
the more miles I fly
nerves setting in
as time passes by

I can't help but think
that isn't it strange
the closer I am to home
the farther I feel away

I found myself in Cali
but here is not so clear
the place I know the best
is full of doubt and fear

I have to block it out
I refuse to let it in
I'm walking in with armor
so let the games begin

when these wheels touch down
they'll still never know
that happy girl I am
living on the west coast.

BIRTHDAY GIFTS PT. II

it was maybe on a thursday
almost my 23rd birthday

friends coming in town
new dress to wear around

my very special day
all the plans perfectly in place

then you call with a surprise
you're going to rehab another time

why'd you have to choose this date
your next adventure couldn't wait

let me break down really quick
grab my dress and all my ~~shit~~

atleast I've heard it all before
I know exactly what's in store

but next time please wait to say
it on a day that's not my day.

to fall or slip
into a former state
you took the step
to seal your fate

all my hope
is falling down
to its former place
on solid ground

don't know what's worse
the first or the last
but it doesn't matter
you'll never ask

I know you're ashamed
feel you failed me again
so the only way to cope
is to numb it from within

to fall or slip
into a former state
you wanted my time
and now it's too late.

BLAME GAME

you've always hated that I love him
you'll deny it but I know you do
your argument is that he left me
I'm pretty sure you left me too

deep inside me
I know it's not fair
how I treat you different
it's blatantly clear

I have a few ideas
why exactly that is
for starters he only
made his problems his

the hurt that he caused
was one deep cut
that's easy to heal
and with time cover up

but yours just keeps cutting
me over again
and you can't heal a wound
that's always open

so there are my reasons
for all the hostility
maybe we could end it
if you took responsibility.

SECURITY BLANKET

I wove a blanket full of anger
it kept me warm with all my rage
it helped me cover all the scars
I had acquired at my young age

so much hatred
so much anguish
I just wanted you to leave
my love was sacred
I watched it vanquish
just as quick as you did me

I refused to let you win
I saw my tears as being weak
I refused to let you break me
so growing cold was my technique

if I don't care then it won't hurt
but what's a teenager to do
when the truth is brought to light
and now I stand here like a fool

I gave you everything I had
more than any child should
you repaid me with your lies
and used me any way you could

so that's how I was raised
thinking that's what mothers do
so excuse me if I'm angry
you see what you put me through?

yes I was hateful
you called it ungrateful
I just blocked out all the pain
cause I was faithful
you were unstable
what I felt was best contained

cause if I melted this ice cold heart of mine
I would destroy us both with vicious words
I'd tell you things you couldn't handle
we would both be smothered by all the hurt

so please continue to call me selfish
for carrying my fiery blanket of rage
I've burned myself protecting you
after everything you're still the one I save.

LET IT BURN

so many fires
I need to put out
there's too many issues
I can't even count

do better for you
not better for me
just get it together
so I can be free

free from the worries
so haunting
so deep
with everyone breaking
you expect me to sleep?

they're constantly breaking
at speeds I can't meet
try to catch falling pieces
shards of glass at my feet

it's heavy
it's hurting
I do the best I can
but there has to come a point
that's more than I can stand

is it self-love or selfish
if I decide to quit
it seems like every passing year
a brand-new fire is lit

do I save myself
or run towards the flame?
if it all burns down
will I carry the blame?

YOU KNOW WHO YOU ARE

I watch the flames rise
I feel someone grab my hand
I look to my side
and I finally understand

the house that's burning
isn't my home
it's in the people I've found
as I walk and I roam

I found refuge in my friends
when my house was filled with strife
they shielded me from darkness
and they truly saved my life

so if all these ~~at one time~~ strangers
can show me so much love
I'd be crazy not to believe
that I am more than enough

I may not be enough
to keep my house safe
but that thing was determined
to burn anyways

I'm just so amazed
in this life that I've found
incredible friends
that fought to pull me out.

they told me blood
is thicker than water
perhaps not the case
for forgotten daughters

how strong are the ties
of the family that bind
when things start to unravel
and you're losing your mind

doubting the stories
they told you about
you question the lessons
you had figured out

that family is strong
a bond made of steel
can never be broken
no wound they can't heal

but when it comes from within
the bond comes undone
those family ties
are coming unspun

when loving them hurts
cause you can't help but try
to be there to save them
to keep them alive

but who's there for you
when you're crying at night
cause your blood is too weak
they've lost will to fight

you're broken. alone.
always looking around
for someone who cares
no one can be found

but it only takes one
to change your whole life
introduce you to love
watch the flame reignite

they stop you from sinking
pull you up from below
that familial darkness
you began to call home

you start to form ties
of unconditional love
not forced by relation
you love just because

they're there without question
you give them your all
when your blood lets you down
they cushion the fall

now I'm stuck choosing sides
of which bond will last
the one I'm born into
or the one found by chance

I'm lost in translation
the words that I've found
cause blood thicker than water
makes it easier to drown.

THICKER THAN WATER PT. II

they told me blood
is thicker than water
when the blood starts to sink
I can't help but wonder

how strong are the ties
of the family that bind
when you're losing your brother
and there's no place to hide

the things that you've known
the lies you've been taught
all go out the window
when you think it's your fault

that family is perfect
an untouchable bond
but when it cracks at the seam
you can barely hold on

from the outside it's pretty
so no one would guess
when you look from inside
it's a miserable mess

when loving them hurts
cause they missed out on life
and you're left all alone
just trying to survive

but who's there for you
when you're hiding your pain
cause to grieve for your loss
might drive you insane

you're angry. alone.
just trying to wake up
from this nightmarish life
you can't cover up

but it only takes one
to change your whole life
make it worth it to love
watch the flame reignite

they stop you from sinking
pull you up from below
that familial darkness
you began to call home

you start to form ties
of unconditional love
do the craziest things
and all just because

they're there when you need them
they'll never give up
when you're afraid to be open
it's worth it to love

now I'm caught in between
these two unique bonds
they told me that blood
would always be strong

but he gave me my life
helped me find solid ground
cause blood thicker than water
made it easier to drown.

A TEAM

sometimes you meet someone
and it doesn't quite work out
but they're the most important love
you could ever live without

I met you in the dark
there was so much you didn't know
but you saw that I was lost
and so you made yourself my home

you brought me in
and made me safe
you held me tight
in your embrace

it only grew
with passing years
loving memories
as souvenirs

as you painted pictures of our future
my ugly past just slipped away
somehow dreaming of our life together
made all the bad just seem okay

I wish this story ended nice
with happily ever after
but you were just too good for me
cause I was still a disaster

you carried all my burdens
at the time I couldn't see
you got weighed down by my issues
that were slowly haunting me

see when you've never felt a love like that
it kills you to let it go
cause a love like yours so beautiful
is one I died to know

I didn't realize what I was doing
I was tearing that love apart
I was your little tornado
wreaking havoc through your heart

I was so selfish
not to see
I was hurting you
like they hurt me

almost 5 years later
from when we met
you shut me out
and I'll never forget

it wasn't right
never meant to be
two different people
wanting different things

you called it quits
you stood your ground
I think I broke you
too far down

you showed me what
it meant to be loved
you saw my worst
yet you never judged

so thank you to
my first true love
I wasn't ready for you
but I'm happy she was.

you showed me true love
taught me I was enough
now that I got my lesson
it's time to pay up

I broke the same heart
more times than deserved
here's a taste of my medicine
my heartbreak is served

to all the cute boys
who don't plan to stay
I'm willing to take it
it's a small price to pay

cause you don't get to break
an innocent heart
with no repercussions
before you restart.

I've been through so much
am I capable of love?
could someone understand
all the wounds I heal from?
how they've shaped me and made me
the person I've become

I'm complex
my heart's in shambles
you want to love me
that's a gamble
but place your bets and be the prince
and I'll surely be the damsel.

so much frustration
from making right choices
there's too many options
too many voices

the battle inside
he says he wants more
must stick to my guns
what I'm fighting for

it's more than fame
or glamour it's power
the choices I make
in this very hour

I know if I start
I won't be able to stop
I won't reach the end
I won't reach the top

so I gather my strength
to say no is hard
the dealer can't win
I must show my cards

it has to get easier
with each hand I show
it has to get easier
every time I say no

when I look at the progress
I feel so strong
like the choices are mine
I sing my own song

I think about the greatness
that I want to become
that level of discipline
can only be done by some

the child in me
wants to cry
the competitor in me
needs to fight

I'm tired of the struggle
I'm sick of the guilt
these weeds grown so tall
it's time that they wilt

this feeling is the battle
that I always give up
no longer a prisoner
this system's corrupt

my body is my kingdom
we're taking him down
not without a fight
but I will regain my crown.

DIG DEEPER

tonight I am full
without reaching capacity
to eat within my limits
it feels so satisfactory

is it possible
that there is hope
to find a way out
a method to cope

mind full of conversation
while they sit around and eat
consuming without a conscience
now that would be a treat

I twirl around my glass
to distract from inner thoughts
to focus on my goals
to step outside the box

the shrinking cube
trying to pull me in
and make me so small
I am fragile again

but this girl can't break
I've found a strength
it was buried deep down
inside of me

tonight that strength
was put to the test
it showed me the potential
to clean up this mess

I believe I can do it
deep in my heart
I am in control
and this is the start.

WORTH IT

maybe I'm always numb
so I can't feel the love
oblivious to the advances
minimize the chances

to feel the hurt
to be let down
to get my hopes up
and watch them come around

chain my heart
so nothing gets in
I've forgotten this feeling
that's stirring again

without it so long
I don't know how to do it
I need some guidance
to help me get through it

it seems so easy
but I make it so hard
what I want is so close
why does it feel far?

I think I don't deserve it
why would they want more?
I always fear they'll leave
when they find out what's in store

I count myself out
don't even let them in
even if they're trying
I won't let myself win

what am I so scared of?
maybe I'm not enough
I always fall too fast
before they feel the love

so I hide myself away
if I don't try I'll never lose
even if they want me
they don't get to choose

cause I don't think I'm worth it
I don't think I've learned yet
maybe in my mind
I don't think I've earned it

I'm scared they'll like the idea of me
and then I'll let them in
I'll open up my heart again
the heart I've tried to mend

the things that we could be
will turn to what we could have been
so I stay selling myself short
I accept just being the friend

always there for support
and anything they need
I'll take care of them
but who takes care of me?

I give all of myself
even as a friend
cause I hope one day
the self-sabotage will end

and I'll be brave enough to say
without fear of defeat
that I deserve to be more
then maybe they'll see

the girl that I could be
right by their side
the one that they hold close
when we're laying there at night

I want that more than anything
I guess I still don't know my worth
to believe someone could want me
is what I have to work on first.

MANNEQUIN

I'm scared you'll read my words
and see me in a different way
but at least you'll see the real me
and not the one that's on display.

BEAUTY IN THE BROKEN

the beauty in the broken
not what it once was
the young and the hopeful
can fall without love

have to take care
to get what they need
young minds are so fragile
like planting the seeds

of how to be loved
or if they're even enough
that like petals they are beauty
but in their roots they are tough

as delicate as a flower
that needs help to grow
without that love and affection
they may not ever know

how to open their hearts
and let someone in
to be true to themselves
so their lives can begin

conditions get tough
and petals grow weak
the beauty is lost
for the answers they seek

but there's beauty in the broken
as the petals grow back
rediscover strength in their roots
and the love they once lacked.

scared of this feeling
the feeling is right
we talk all day long
and lay there all night

you needed the release
something we both know
I needed the affection
I tried not to show

talked from minutes turned to hours
into the new day
from the daylight into darkness
and welcoming new rays

I immediately knew
I was going down a road
that's dangerous for me
has such a tight hold

not because it's bad
or has danger in sight
but because I'm afraid
of all the feelings I fight

I try so hard to get close
I hope and I pray
but as distance gets smaller
I always run away

I'm scared to get hurt
to let someone in
cause what if I want more
and they just want to be friends

so I tell myself these stories
how it couldn't be true
"that's not what he meant"
"he'd never like you"

I always give up
before I've even began
I always let him go
in the past I've always ran

what if I face it?
what if I try?
I'm scared of what he'll say
I'm scared he'll blow my high

if I just stay here in limbo
I guess I'll never know
but if I hang in limbo here
my heart just might stay whole

this is why I hate these feelings
they consume all of my mind
if I actually told the truth
it might consume my time

so I think I'll be a coward
and pretend it doesn't exist
I want to open up
but I'm scared to take that risk

will I ever love again?
will I let anyone in?
too scared to be rejected
to be let down again
we could be so much more
but we'll probably just stay friends.

hoping the next time
won't be the last
what if I fall?
I might just crash

others had my heart
a few times before
but this time it's different
undoubtedly something more

connected on all levels
I didn't know exist
disconnecting from my fear
would be the biggest risk

can't predict the reaction
can't imagine the response
fully putting myself out there
would be unorthodox

so I live in fear
hiding away
processing the words
I know I'll never say

I don't know how you feel
so I hold it all in
just enjoying our time
never wanting it to end

I push then I pull
too scared to go too far
so I sit in silent longing
like the time we talked to stars

he told me we were soulmates
to the world it'd make no sense
but yet I needed to tell you
somehow I let you in

never to judge
always to be
you make me feel safe
you make me feel free

you've taken me to places
I would not have believed
we've opened our eyes
to things we can't see

changed for better
you push me to grow
we build each other up
but still we don't know

what are we doing?
what does this mean?
do we give in to doubts
or dare to be seen?

for the true souls we are
and what we might feel
to put it all out there
would make it so real

but that's what we need
some moments of truth
that fearless mentality
we lost from our youth

I need all the courage
to muster some strength
can't pretend forever
can't hide what I seek

how to put it in words
or choose the right time
when did being so honest
become such a crime

I have to let go
of all expectations
live in the moment
of every situation

how to be honest
how to be true
how to simply say
"hey I think I like you"

so many human questions
can mess it all up
to trust my emotions
that should be enough

God says he has a plan
so I need to have faith
trust him wholeheartedly
to know that I am safe

to go out on a limb
expose my inner thoughts
to share with you those feelings
this whole time I have fought

I'll try to get them out
share what's on my heart
and if you also feel it
it could be a beautiful start.

FOREIGN LOVE

drawn together
like a magnetic force
walking side by side
two souls one course

lifting each other
higher and higher
every conversation
I leave more inspired

to be a better version
of the person I was
to open my heart
and explore all the love

easy to speak
but nervous to touch
want to give my all
but not be too much

the feelings inside
are so hard to show
in a way you'll understand
in a way you'll truly know

cause when love has become
so distant and foreign
feeling the truth in my affection
is of utmost importance

one day I'll give in
and let my insecurities go
make you feel what I feel
because you deserve to know
deserve to be shown
deserve to be close.

a multitude of questions
confusion on display
a scarcity in answers
what we lack in what we say

feel the tension rise and fall
we catch and we release
flames lit inside put out
a cold and bitter tease

but there's a need to play this game
connection stays alive
we live in longing limbo
but in this place we thrive

it doesn't make sense
can't be understood
wouldn't want to explain
if even we could

should we let it be
and never know
or risk it all
to see it grow

a mind full of questions
confusion on display
a scarcity in honesty
what we lack in what we say.

.

love is alive
and it's fighting to grow
our minds keep it captive
we're scared of the unknown

love set free
is an unstoppable force
love trapped by doubt
is forever in the dark.

what's so hard
about letting it out
all the great things
you have me thinking about

if I was yours
if you were mine
to take that risk
to cross that line

so much pain stems
from my fear
but I'd give anything
to have you here

with you I'm safe
no care in the world
when I'm next to you
just a boy and a girl

taking on this journey
two paths into one
it's a lot more simple
it brings out the fun

I know you so well
it doesn't make sense
how we've grown so close
but still keep distance

both so scared
afraid to be loved
is it really ourselves
that we're terrified of

afraid to be open
to let someone in
cause if my heart is exposed
it might get hurt again

but just like he said
we don't rise we fall
falling into the unknown
and risking it all

it's how we feel
the greatest joys in life
by first fighting through
the walls we build inside

so many things
I'm dying to say
some I haven't told myself
just pushing them away

cause if I'm honest with myself
and acknowledge the truth
it makes it real
then there's something to lose

can't lose a love
that you never had
so I avoid all my feelings
as if they were bad.

how could something
so beautiful and true
be pushed down to the depths
no light to seep through

I want love to grow
but keep it out of the light
you can't see the beauty
when it's kept out of sight

are you ashamed?
is it ugly?
reasons you hide away
or are you just too selfish
to put the truth in what you say?

to shield love away
should be the biggest crime
you're denying the blessings
rejecting the divine

letting insecurities
stand in my own way
sabotaging myself
wondering why I'm not okay

is the pit in my stomach
worth not speaking up
when all I really want
is to feel his love

if that's truly what I want
there's only one path
that's the only way to get it
the only chance I have

so first it's being honest
what I feel
what I want
then figuring out the way
to get what I've sought

and I have a feeling
the only way out
is to express my feelings
without fear
without doubt

but just like any task
you know where you want to end
you take the right steps
and let the journey begin

so why is this different?
they're one in the same
cause you see what you want
but it's a more dangerous game

you risk getting hurt
and feeling real pain
but if you keep it all inside
you'll probably go insane

so I must be honest with myself
what do I want?
then be honest again
about all the things I've thought

if I finally let it out
and it's what I want to hear
so much stress is relieved
I'll have conquered my fears

but if the response I get
isn't what I had hoped
I'll still be relieved
not walking this tight rope

so here goes nothing
let's start with me
expressing how I feel
with full honesty.

COMPLICATED

a complicated mess
I've found myself in
quarrels between lovers
or fights between friends

he's so full of ~~shit~~
but I can't let him go
cause losing sight of him
means losing sight of home

he makes wrong decisions
knowing darn well what's right
frustration when he tells me
understanding by the night

we started out as strangers
just a friend of another friend
but somehow our paths stayed crossed
and now there's a heart to mend

grew too close for friendship
but that's a truth we'll never tell
mainly to ourselves
the biggest lie we'll ever sell

we can't go forward
just not right now
we can't go back
don't even know how

both so unsure
of what to do
this random piece of my heart
I've given to you

I gave it without thinking
and I can't get it back
no matter what you do
it's still yours that's a fact

I feel the connection
the memories that bind
in the clues left in our past
our future we will find

it is the fool who avoids
denies all that's inside
you think you've locked it up
you can run but you can't hide

it is the fool who pretends
that love does not exist
then cries at random parties
from opportunities they've missed

at some point I say no more
to the history I repeat
in the problems of my past
I won't find the answers that I seek

I was honest told the truth
checked my heart there's still a beat
I let it out broke the dam
all of my feelings I release

lifting weight off of my back
my spine is growing strong
guess I stood up for myself
regaining my backbone

even if you're not prepared
to take that same large leap
the thoughts I planted in your head
are the seeds that I will reap

so many words still left unsaid
they're running through your brain
you don't have to tell me all right now
you wait too long my mind might change

all the things I don't expect
to see from us right now
but if this thing is meant to be
it could happen someday. somehow.

STUPID

trying so hard
have to play it right
but the insecurities
make it hard to sleep at night

being so close
to what you want so bad
but the closer that you get
more fear that it won't last

I'm being stupid
words are useless
cause I'm holding it all in

to the world I'm fearless
but he'll never feel this
cause I'm scared to let him in

but again I'm stupid
attempts are useless
I'm the one who let it begin

the first kiss was magic
the spark said it all
a passion you can't deny
knew I was bound to fall

I get so angry
no one can save me
from the thoughts inside my head

let's take it slowly
I want you only
when I'm safe with you in bed

can it be simple?
can I just trust it?
I'm gonna ruin this again

know I'm not meant to
can I just love it?
the process of diving in

I'm in the deep end
gotta sink or swim
will I just take the easy way out?

will I believe it?
all that I see from him
or will I helplessly watch myself drown?

when will I make a change
not wonder what to say
not be afraid to open up

find value in what I feel
not be too scared to say what's real
when will the darkness be enough

don't let it linger
you must forget her
the broken girl you were before

cause now you're stronger
and I wonder
what the new me has in store.

GOOD BOYS

I don't like letting
good things in
each time I do
they leave again

so I chase after boys
that don't want to be loved
so I won't be surprised
when they finally give up

I don't like letting
good boys in
they could love me or leave me
and that I can't predict.

HANG AGAIN SOON

I don't understand
what I'm doing that's wrong
avoiding the signs
that I saw all along

I'm trying too hard
not trying enough
this road isn't simple
it's bumpy
it's rough

I'm trying it all
thinking something will work
"let's hang again soon"
he says with a smirk

now I've heard this before
but it didn't pan out
I waited to see him
but just got let down

"let's hang again soon"
you're proposing a plan
a boy full of ~~shit~~
one thing I can't stand

I use to be sad
but now I'm annoyed
this isn't a game
and I'm not some cute toy

so say what you mean
and mean what you say
if you want to hang out
then let's set a date

and now I feel petty
just like a little girl
trying to figure out
how to navigate this world

but forget it
it's true
I don't understand
how I come up for a boy
when I look for a man

I thought so long
that maybe it's me
but now that I've grown
I fully disagree

with so much to give
and so much within
it doesn't make sense
how I'm back here again

searching for love
trying to shape who I am
having same conversations
I don't think I can

so this one is it
it's all up to you
"let's hang again soon"
I hope you follow through.

love has no limits
they can not exist
to try to contain it
is man's biggest risk

holding it in
when it wants to be free
the limits we create
the only ones there can be

whether rooted in fear
or insecurity
the limits we create
kill possibility.

OCEAN EYES PT. 1

waking up
to ocean eyes
take it slow
let the sun rise

soft fingertips
caress your skin
the lightest touch
as the light flows in

half asleep
but wake enough
can't take my eyes off
this man I love

silent mornings
lost in bed
the sea of sheets
where we lay our heads

keeping quiet
no need for sound
laying so close
I feel your heart pound

we rest here
face to face
as if it's the last time
we'll be in this place

I always look forward
to the time I'm there next
gazing into ocean eyes
as I lay on your chest.

what am I to you?
tell me what I mean
is this all just a game?
am I even on your team?

I'm going out on limbs
pushing myself to the seams
trying to figure your life out
I'm just stuck here in between

full frustration setting in
but it's mostly made of pain
keep pouring my emotions
watch them circle down the drain

give me something
open up
just a little
still no luck

don't need too much
there's just a lack
of the words
holding you back

you have my heart
so please take care
it's pretty fragile
please be aware

didn't mean to give it
it happened either way
so tell me if you want it
that's all you have to say.

CONSTANT WAVE

am I fooling myself?
or do I look like a fool?
could be neither one
or both of the two

say I have no expectations
just take it day by day
but if he asked me how I felt
I don't know what I'd say

am I a fool to fall in love
too naïve to see the truth
am I telling myself stories
so in the end it's me and you

go through bouts where I don't care
feeling free when all is good
then I find doubt and I get scared
that you might leave because you could

push me out
then pull me in
a constant wave
that never ends

and now it's funny
at times you'll say
you'll take me surfing
but that's every day

we ride this wave
of you and me
what if that's all
we'll ever be.

ocean eyes
take a dip inside
swimming through the blue
so clear that I can't hide

ocean eyes
I got caught up again
trying to fight the current
now it's time to sink or swim

ocean eyes
the ones I tell my lies
I know that you see through me
but I hope you realize

if I'm honest
I'd tell you what I think
I'd show you all these notions
that are flipping in my brain

if I'm honest
I'd tell you you're enough
tell you that you're perfect
even when you're at your worst

but I won't be honest
cause I'm scared of what you'll say
been down that road before
that's a ride that I can't take.

no words
silence
no romance
slow dance
no contact
resistance
no crying
appearance
no hoping
acceptance
no weakness
endurance
no movement
stagnance
no closeness
distance
no thinking
avoidance

these are the rules
new stance
these are the terms
no chance
these are the guidelines
and ultimately our consequence.

SAND IN HANDS

I'm on the edge waiting
ready for his way out
mental prepping for the let down
can't love without doubt

decided to love
to give it my all
accepted my fate
I chose to fall

I'd choose to love
than just be numb
this was my past
but I won't run

if he does leave
I'll wish him well
he's changed my life
that's why I fell

no rhyme or reason
to believe it
that he might just walk away
but if I see it
before the season
there's a chance I'll be okay

I'll let you in
on my big secret
a heart to hold
is what I don't believe in

it slips away
like sand in hands
you try to catch it
but never can.

CYNIC

I don't like to
think this way
to be a cynic
full of dismay

but I've loved and lost
from way too young
I learned a different
version of love

a short time
not a lifetime
no matter who you are
and if nothing lasts forever
am I just wishing on a star?

everything moves
in slow motion now
it's falling apart
and I can't fathom how

is he scared?
was this fake?
many thoughts in my head
when the phone rings tonight
it's his name that I dread

I don't want this to end
no way this is right
had no clue how he felt
a total blindside

praying for a chance
to please let me in
have faith in the future
don't let the past win

but I'm fully aware
it's out of my control
I only can try
to keep myself whole.

ACTIONS SPEAK

let it grow
or need to know
how you feel
you let it show

your actions speak
when words cannot
they tell me things
they say a lot

but a worried mind
does hold me back
shows all the things
I've always lacked

confidence
in me and you
need to calm my mind
to get me through

why must you spell
it out with words
in all you did
I should have heard

don't use my mind
but use my heart
to let you go
now that's a start.

SUNRISE

love dies
like the night sky
with the sunrise
upon closed eyes
my tears dried
but my heart cries
why?

where did you go
do you think of me
I'll never know
from your heart no
words flow
so now I am alone
why?

was it all a game
was I just the same
could you feel the flame
or was I just insane
why?

can't get you out of my head
want you in my bed
but now it's over
dead
why?

cause love dies
like the night sky
with the sunrise.

STAY FRIENDS PT. II

just as I suspected
I decided to let you in
but you decided for yourself
you just wanted to be my friend

and for a few weeks
I cannot lie
my pillow will tell you
I cried and I cried

I let myself feel
I let myself heal
cause what I felt for you
was always real

turns out I was the one
who needed space
time heals all wounds
and reveals all mistakes

see I wasn't wrong
for wanting you
I still laugh
about the things we'd do

but I lost myself
along the way
and that right there
was my mistake

I wanted the things
that we could be
but ignored red flags
in front of me

shed layers of my worth
to fit into a mold
that I created myself
out of silver and gold

but when I took a step back
I opened my eyes
I fought to win you over
but I was the prize

I wanted so much
but I was settling for less
and everything I needed
I already possessed

I lost sight of how
to be treated like a queen
and most importantly
I lost sight of me

but baby I'm back
and this is where our story ends
so I couldn't agree more
we should definitely just stay friends.

STAY FRIENDS PT. III

see that's the thing
about being my friend
you don't get treated
like you did back then

all the loving things
I did just for you
to make you feel special
are over and through

those things are reserved
for the man that I'm with
that's no longer you
and you made sure of this

so now just be my friend
there are lines we don't cross
and the next man I love
will gain from your loss.

ASK YOURSELF

from now on
with any new potential
I'll ask this question
my new dating essential

this question directed
at me myself and I
do you like yourself better
or worse by his side

be brutal
be honest
rose tinted glasses gone
and truly assess
what's right and what's wrong

is he deserving of the person
you've finally grown to be
if your dad knew how he acted
would he say that he's worthy

realize you have the choice
but don't live in the dream
cause if the answer to the question's "no"
then queen it's time to leave.

ACT

I just now realized
as I'm laying in my bed
I decided to be an actress
cause that's all I ever did

act like an adult
when you're barely in your teens
act like you're put together
as you're ripping at the seams

act like a teen
do all the things girls your age do
act like your parent
teach yourself lessons you never knew

act like life is beautiful
like you desperately want it to be
and if you do it well enough
maybe even you'll believe.

PLAY PRETEND

sometimes I decide
to let you back in
to feel like a child
let's play pretend

pretending I have you
like nothing went wrong
pretend I never lost you
you were there all along

I just want to chat
maybe gossip 'bout a boy
get nails done and shop
all the things we enjoy

I always know that it won't last
I stopped believing that it would
I'm not naïve I'm just a girl
who plays pretend just like I should.

DOORS PT. II

opportunity knocking
just answer the door
sorry wrong person
who are you looking for?

they knock
I run
to answer it quick
the door won't open
it needs to be fixed

to let them in
not keep them out
this is my life
they're knocking about

we sit and wait
and hope for a sound
at the end of most days
we end up let down

to wait at the door
like a dog for its man
we'd get up and go
we wish that we can

but the leash is too short
you can't go too far
cause the day that door opens
it could make you a star.

EXHAUSTION

exhaustion setting in
I feel the wear and tear
my mind is going numb
a face with a blank stare

so much to do
so little time
to do it all
I sacrifice

a good night's sleep
a fun night out
the Hollywood life
they all rave about

I take my time
I map it out
distribute it all
from north to south

it slips my mind
to factor in
the hours for me
to breathe again

time is money
money is time
to get to the top
you have to climb

higher and higher
to get to your peak
oxygen levels dropping
it's harder to breathe

do you continue to climb
when you can't see the top
too exhausted to continue
too stubborn to stop

cue the blank stare
out at the view
when all you're searching for
is inside of you

I gather my strength
whether real or believed
to keep pushing on
I must move my feet

if they say that it's easy
they've never been there
on the way to the top
you're tired
you're scared

trying to find a reason
to keep pushing on
to give them a reason
that you do belong

so I keep my head up
when it's pulling me down
the exhaustion might win
but only this round

if I stay in the ring
and battle this out
it will all be worth it
every challenge I've found.

GRATEFUL FOR THE SUN

I'm grateful for the sun
that opens my eyes
touches my skin
and gives me life

the warming touch
like someone you love
the radiant feeling
can swallow you up

I remind myself
of how much I have
and all of the people
without even half

of the blessings I see
the people I love
opportunities I get
that most would dream of

I'm living my dream
sometimes it gets hard
but because of those people
I have to go far

to live my dreams
for the ones who can not
to raise my voice
for the ones who have fought

to feel that sunrise
on their skin
to know that
they're alive again.

to my brother up in heaven
I wish I could've watched you grow
but you will never be forgotten
and that's all you need to know

I live life to the fullest
cause you never got the chance
I'll make you proud and reach my dreams
for that I thank you in advance

I'll be the coolest big sister
I'll travel to far away lands
so one day when we meet again
you'll hold the whole world in your hands

two promises now
before I go
keep them close
and call them home

I promise to keep you
alive in my heart
I promise to cherish
this life
every part

cause the only promise
that can't be made
is that I get to see
another day.

I'll always be
daddy's little girl
you're the most important
person in my world

maybe it's because
I always wished
I could see you more
all the memories we missed

I got excited
at the slightest
chance to see you
that life provided

I remember moments
not too many
but they're my favorites
I felt less empty

I got my sense
of humor from you
I chase my dreams
cause that's what you do

I've spent every day
since the day that you left
still missing you dearly
but crying way less

cause your love for me
I can never deny
you brag about me often
I think I keep you alive

so daddy I'll always
be your little girl
when life got dark
you always lit up my world.

I'm here brother
are you there?
there's no need
to be so scared

I've felt your pain
I've walked this path
it isn't pretty
but it doesn't last

so please be strong
I'm here for you
I've fought my battles
and I'll fight yours too

right by your side
we're standing strong
I'll have your back
whether right or wrong

if there's one thing
that I can say
you are enough
and that won't change

you are enough
you are loved
you are never alone
any time you feel weak
just pick up the phone

I'm here for you brother
any day and every night
so let me be your armor
when you've lost will to fight

I know that you have questions
I can handle one or two
but where you'll find your answers
is deep inside of you

our parents are not heroes
just humans like me and you
and if you ask me why they broke us
maybe cause they were broken too.

CYCLES

you broke me
but she broke you
this cyclical sadness
is nothing new

I may not get your actions
but I understand your pain
when you feel your mother's love
isn't easily obtained

took 24 years
to finally see
your problems were so much
older than me

I was always enough
the child you wanted to love
your angel sent from above
but you couldn't keep up

the past pulled you down
took every chance that it found
it'll drag you around
and some day into the ground

but as I own my past
I know it to be
this cyclical sadness
will end with me.

the things you believe
are not as they seem
the world you live in
has crushed your self-esteem

withheld love
and a parent who's left
the only one you needed
you've tried your very best

I need to tell you
it isn't your fault
you didn't cause this pain
you feel in your heart

it comes from the wounds
that parents still tend
wrapped up in themselves
no loving hand to lend

you've taken their burdens
and never by choice
felt out of your control
no silence in the noise

I need you to know
you are amazing beyond belief
a true light to this world
in the dark you can't see

it doesn't mean it's not there
it will always shine through
the world will feel your light
no matter what you do

right now I know
it's hard to understand
you can't see the purpose
the whole master plan

you were made so special
there's so much ahead
believe in yourself
have faith where you're led

you feel you're not enough
cause you couldn't make them stay
but it was the power of the drugs
that pulled them far away.

a therapy
a remedy
an easy way out
for the hard parts of life
feeling lost and never found

a treatment
a fix
a light at the end
giving me hope
a reason to live

not to sound morbid
like I'd physically die
but it ignites my soul
and makes me feel alive

it's like knowing the reason
why you've felt all your pain
and using those moments
to help you feel sane

the fuel to my purpose
is the life that I've had
partly the good
but mostly the bad

I didn't know then
the things I know now
I couldn't see why
didn't understand how

when I was young and alone
without the love that I needed
I always told myself
everything happens for a reason

I didn't know what it was
but I had to believe
that there was a purpose
and one day I'd see

my therapy
my remedy
my easy way out
the things that I write
the stories I've found

my fix
my treatment
my light at the end
my art is my love
my lifelong friend.

MY LIGHT

looking up to me
watch me lead
the hardest steps
they may not see

putting pressure
on the diamond rough
make it stronger
make it tough

shine on
keep calm
it's the calm
before the storm

I inspire
lift them higher
can't give up
even when you're tired

such an honor
to hear their words
they make me free
like a cageless bird

give permission
to spread my wings
they heard my cries
the caged bird sings

bringing tears
assessing fears
beliefs that held me
for many years

these new faces
I've never known
have seen the spark
have watched me grow

once a stranger
now a friend
getting closer
now my kin

so much love
it fills my heart
flows from the cup
that is my art

creative minds
colored outside the lines
believed in my purpose
they opened my eyes

to who I could be
things I could do
when I got out the way
and fear didn't rule

to this group of people
who have built me up
no thanks in the world
could ever be enough

for the people you are
the things that you do
you look up to me
I look up to you

the highest praise
I could ever receive
you help me inspire
because you make me believe

that this angel
once with broken wings
could achieve so much
could reach her dreams

each fracture mended
one at a time
until one day
I happened to find

pieces back together
no reason to cry
my heart was healing
and I realized why

it's not about the people
who've hurt you in the past
it's about the strange faces
that become familiar fast

who shower you with love
that's always unconditional
and help you keep faith
when life is unpredictable

the past isn't as dark
when the future seems so bright
so thank you to those people
you've all become my light.

MOSAIC

you're a mosaic
a masterpiece
quite the work of art
all the pieces placed back together
much like a broken heart

once complete
you gleamed perfection
then someone broke you
something wrecked you

shattered pieces
all around
with sharpened edges
once smooth and round

flawless and harmless
now disfigured with pain
your biggest fear
the imperfections remain

we've all been broken
can't escape it
glue the pieces together
look what you've created

you're a mosaic
stitched together
love and care at every seam
so find beauty in the broken
cause it makes you more unique.

so the details weren't pretty
but the story truly is
an angel dragged through hell and back
and still she chose to live

pretty me
so pretty be
but now you know
the full story

the pretty lies
between the lines
of ugly stories
a nice disguise

so if I'm pretty
then so are you
once you accept
your story is too.

Made in the USA
Columbia, SC
10 June 2021